Wave Pools

Precious McKenzie

rourkeeducationalmedia.com

Scan for Related Titles
and Teacher Resources

Teaching Focus: Using Models

To demonstrate that simple models can be used to represent real world objects that are not easily brought into a classroom.

Before Reading:

Building Academic Vocabulary and Background Knowledge

Before reading a book, it is important to set the stage for your child or student by using pre-reading strategies. This will help them develop their vocabulary, increase their reading comprehension, and make connections across the curriculum.

1. *Read the title and look at the cover. Let's make predictions about what this book will be about.*
2. *Take a picture walk by talking about the pictures/photographs in the book. Implant the vocabulary as you take the picture walk. Be sure to talk about the text features such as headings, the Table of Contents, glossary, bolded words, captions, charts/diagrams, or index.*
3. *Have students read the first page of text with you then have students read the remaining text.*
4. *Strategy Talk – use to assist students while reading.*
   - *Get your mouth ready*
   - *Look at the picture*
   - *Think…does it make sense*
   - *Think…does it look right*
   - *Think…does it sound right*
   - *Chunk it – by looking for a part you know*
5. *Read it again.*
6. *After reading the book, complete the activities below.*

Content Area Vocabulary
Use glossary words in a sentence.

chlorinated
dissipates
energy
frequency
pressure
system

After Reading:

Comprehension and Extension Activity

After reading the book, work on the following questions with your child or students in order to check their level of reading comprehension and content mastery.

1. *Why do you think wave pools are filled with chlorinated water? (Summarize)*
2. *How many gallons of water does it take to make a wave in a wave pool? (Asking questions)*
3. *In science, how is a wave defined? (Text to self connection)*
4. *Why would surfers use a wave pool? (Summarize)*

Extension Activity

Make your own wave pool! After reading the book, split up into groups of 4 or 5. Set out several 9x13 inch baking pans, and several pitchers or measuring cups filled with water. Fill a pan about half full with water. Then ask the members of your group, "What is one way we could make waves in our wave pool?" Some possible answers may include rocking or sloshing the pan, blowing on the pan, splashing with your hands. Explore these ideas and see if you can come up with more ways to make waves!

Table of Contents

Wild Pools

Are you looking for an exciting place to cool off on a hot day? Then it's time to visit a wave pool!

Wave-making machines turn ordinary pools into wave pools.

Just like swimming pools, wave pools are filled with **chlorinated** water and have concrete floors and walls.

Wave pools recreate the type of waves you find in the ocean. Sometimes people practice surfing in **wave pools.**

Wave pools can hold about 2 million gallons (7.6 million liters) of water.

Making Waves

Wave-making machines create the waves for swimmers.

In a large wave pool, a wave machine dumps water into the deepest end of the pool.

The water rushes to the shallow end of the pool. This makes the wave.

shallow

deep

It takes about 90,000 gallons (341,000 liters) of water to make a wave in a wave pool. A complex **system** of machines is needed to move all of this water so quickly.

In the ocean, most waves are created by the wind.

The Mechanics

Wave pools have large pumps that force air into a chamber. This **pressure** quickly forces the water out into the pool, creating a wave.

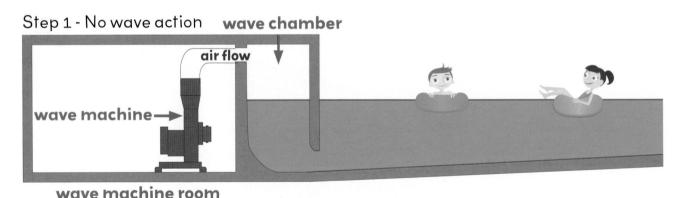

Step 1 - No wave action

wave chamber

air flow

wave machine →

wave machine room

Step 2 - Wave action begins. Air is pumped into chambers that push water down and out into the pool. This makes energy and creates waves in the pool.

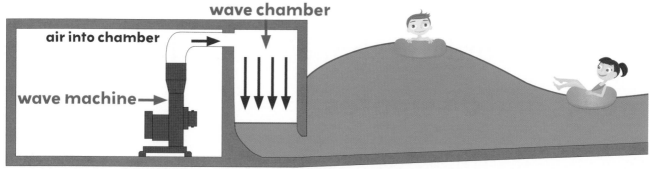

Step 3 - Air is exhausted from chambers, allowing the water level to rise within the chambers.

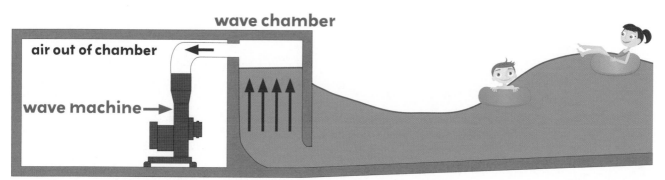

13

When the **energy** travels through the water, it creates waves. The wave energy moves toward the shallow end where it breaks and **dissipates**.

In science, a wave is defined as a transfer of energy. Waves like those in the ocean or a wave pool are called mechanical waves. The water moves up and down, and the energy travels with the wave.

Have Some Fun!

Now the fun begins for the swimmers!

Waves rush across the pool.

Wave height and **frequency** are always a surprise for the swimmers. But both are controlled by the machine and its operators.

Wave pools are not just for kids and families.

Surfers use wave pools too. At surf parks, professional surfers can practice. And, people new to the sport can learn.

On a hot summer day, take a trip to a wave pool.

Have a blast splashing through the
rolling waves!

Photo Glossary

 **chlorinated** (KLOR-uh-NAY-tuhd): Water is chlorinated by adding the chemical chlorine. This is done to kill any germs that might be in the water.

 **dissipates** (diss-uh-PATES): When a wave dissipates, it spreads out and disappears, sometimes at the shoreline or beach.

 **energy** (EN-ur-jee): In science, energy means the power or ability to do work.

 **frequency** (FREE-kwuhn-see): The number of times something happens.

 **pressure** (PRESH-ur): Pressure is the force that is produced by pressing on something.

 **system** (SISS-tuhm): A system is an organized, complex group of parts or machines that work together.

Index

Websites to Visit

www.enchantedlearning.com/subjects/ocean/Waves.shtml

http://kidshealth.org/kid/watch/out/swim.html

http://science.howstuffworks.com/engineering/structural/wave-pool5.htm

About the Author

Precious McKenzie lives in Montana with her husband and three children. She loves swimming and visiting water parks across the United States.

Meet The Author!
www.meetREMauthors.com

© 2017 Rourke Educational Media

www.rourkeeducationalmedia.com

PHOTO CREDITS: Cover ©mdmilliman (girl), ©Steirus (pool); title page, 23: Public Domain; 4-5, 22: ©Darios44; 6: ©Ninelittle; 7: ©Susan Chiang; 8, 9, 14, 15, 22, 23: Courtesy of Murphys Waves Ltd; 10: ©Pieter Kuiper; 11: ©ChrisVanLennepPhoto; 12-13: Jennifer Thomas; 16-17, 22: ©Subhadeepmanna; 18: ©Royalbroil/Wikipedia; 19: ©Greta6; 20: ©Mark Peeler; 21: ©SimplyCreativePhotography

Edited by: Keli Sipperley
Cover and Interior Design by: Jen Thomas

Library of Congress PCN Data

Wave Pools / Precious McKenzie
(How It Works)
ISBN 978-1-68191-683-5 (hard cover)(alk. paper)
ISBN 978-1-68191-784-9 (soft cover)
ISBN 978-1-68191-883-9 (e-Book)
Library of Congress Control Number: 2016932559

Printed in the United States of America, North Mankato, Minnesota

Also Available as:

ROURKE'S